20th Century Defences in Britain
in Britain
Kent

David Burridge was born and lives in Dover, Kent. He is Area Co-ordinator (South East) of the Defence of Britain Project. Involved with a variety of defence heritage groups in the Kent area, he is editor and producer of the journal of the Kent Defence Research Group, of which he is secretary. His previous publications include *The Dover Turret – Admiralty Pier Fort* and *A Guide to the Western Heights Defences, Dover,* and he is a regular contributor to *Bygone Kent*.

20th Century Defences in Britain

Kent

DAVID BURRIDGE

BRASSEY'S

LONDON • WASHINGTON

First English Edition 1997

UK editorial offices: Brassey's, 33 John Street, London WC1N 2AT
UK orders: Marston Book Services, PO Box 269, Abingdon, OX14 4SD

North American orders: Brassey's Inc., PO Box 960,
Herndon, VA 20172

David Burridge has asserted his moral right to be identified as
the author of this work.

Library of Congress Cataloging in Publication Data
Burridge, David, 1947-
Twentieth century defences in Kent/David Burridge. -- 1st English ed.
p. cm.
Includes bibliographical references and index.
ISBN 1-85753-233-3 (flexicover)
1. Kent (England)--History, Military. 2. Fortification--England--Kent--History--20th century.
3. Kent (England)--Defenses.
I Title.
DA670. K3B925 1997
355.7'09422'3--dc21

British Library Cataloguing in Publication Data
A catalogue record for this book is available from the British Library

ISBN 1 85753 233 3 flexicover

Designed and typeset by Simon Ray-Hills
Printed in Hong Kong by Midas Printing Ltd

Cover shows slab sound mirror; Abbot's Cliff, near Capel

CONTENTS

INTRODUCTION

*T*he books in this series have all been compiled by enthusiasts and amateur historians concerned that the military legacy of the twentieth century in the United Kingdom should be recorded. Together, the books provide a basic introduction to an immense and varied aspect of our recent national experience which, for all its fascination, is only now beginning to capture the public imagination.

There can be few people in the British Isles who have observed the remnants of coastal artillery batteries, the windswept expanses of abandoned airfields or the rusting stumps of derelict radar stations without a degree of curiosity. These sites, once central to brief but dramatic episodes in our national history, were often constructed in haste and abandoned without thought once their immediate purpose was fulfilled. In recent years, many have been obliterated and many more will succumb in the future to inexorable urban development or the ravages of time. For the most part, they are not objects of intrinsic beauty, but without exception they are witnesses to the turbulent record of this century. A few are the subjects of authoritative research, many more may be traced through lengthy enquiries into official records, but until recently there has been no central index to guide or inform conservation strategies. It was to meet this need that **The Defence of Britain** project was launched in April 1995.

The Defence of Britain is an ambitious and wholly unique project. Ambitious because coastal batteries, airfields and radar stations are but a small sample of the sites and structures associated with military defence in the twentieth century. Add to these the armaments factories, depots, hospitals, training facilities, prisoner-of-war camps and command installations associated with modern warfare and the list becomes immense. By the conclusion of the project, it is estimated that close to 500,000 sites will have been recorded, ranging from Brennan torpedo launch rails of 1887–1902 to Regional Seats of Government abandoned after the Cold War. This is the raw material of military archaeology, an emergent discipline which awaits wider recognition as industrial archaeology awaited it some 40 years ago.

The project is unique because in order to achieve its daunting objectives it combines the product of conventional academic research with the efforts of amateur societies and volunteer fieldworkers. Many of these groups and individuals have compiled extensive private records and it was partly to acknowledge this work that this series was commissioned. Since the project's launch, their ranks have been swollen by over 3,000 enthusiasts who expressed interest, offered information, subscribed to a quarterly newsletter, bought the project's handbook or attended seminars and day schools run by one of eight regional volunteer co-ordinators. Overseas correspondents have written from Germany, Australia, the United States, Austria and Canada. In Malta, a sister project using similar methodology was launched in 1996.

A project of this size has many technical and administrative hurdles to cross in its first year. Apart from the willing assistance of volunteers, **The Defence of Britain** has benefited from an Advisory Panel representing almost every major heritage organisation in the United Kingdom. A full list of participating bodies appears at the end of this

Introduction but three merit particular mention now. The Council for British Archaeology (CBA) supplies the project not only with administrative support but also with technical expertise in defining terminology and in database design. Fund-raising, always a pressing consideration, is conducted under the umbrella of the CBA in its capacity as a registered charity and 'unlocks' matching funds from the Department of National Heritage and the Heritage Lottery Fund. The Imperial War Museum provides archive and office space at its site on Duxford Airfield, near Cambridge. English Heritage contributes advice and information arising from the Monuments Protection Programme.

Archaeology has more than once been described as a vendetta rather than a profession; it is perhaps a tribute to the voluntary sector that **The Defence of Britain** has brought so many organisations together in successful pursuit of a common purpose.

So what of the future? Clearly, the number of abandoned military sites and buildings will increase dramatically as the armed forces adjust to the end of the Cold War. Some of the most prestigious – the former Royal Naval Staff College at Greenwich and Eltham Palace among them – have already been adopted by other institutions and will be put to alternative use. Many more, particularly those with limited architectural appeal, face an uncertain future in the hands of private owners or developers. Information compiled by **The Defence of Britain** project will ensure that the history of these sites is preserved for future generations, even though the buildings themselves may be demolished or altered beyond recognition.

Equally clearly, the generations who built and manned our national defences wish to record their story. **The Defence of Britain** project is steadily acquiring reminiscences, diaries, photographs and video footage which give a human dimension to the stark relics of war and prepare the way for fresh interpretations of our recent history. It is a continuing process and one which may eventually colour or even demolish many long-held perceptions.

For this reason, none of the contributors to this series would regard it as definitive. Its purpose is to increase awareness of a neglected aspect of our heritage and to emphasise the diversity of military relics which even a casual observer might note on a journey through Britain. The project is always looking for new volunteers who can verify or augment documentary research and if perusal of this volume inspires a new enthusiasm, or even a passing interest, we would be glad to hear from you *(see below for contact details).*

The Defence of Britain project is overseen by representatives of the Association of County Archaeological Officers, Cadw (Welsh Historic Monuments), the Council for British Archaeology, the Council for Scottish Archaeology, the Department of the Environment Northern Ireland, English Heritage, the Fortress Study Group, Historic Scotland, the Imperial War Museum, the Ministry of Defence, the Public Record Office, the Royal Commission on the Historical Monuments of England, the Royal Commission on the Ancient and Historical Monuments of Scotland, and the Royal Commission on the Ancient and Historical Monuments of Wales.

Editor's Note:

For ease of reference, place names and sites in Kent appear initially in bold type. Grid references of some representative sites are provided, by category, in the Gazetteer.

All grid references in this publication are taken from sheets 177, 178, 179, 188, 189 and 199 of the Ordnance Survey 'Landranger' series.

For further information, please write to: **The Defence of Britain project, Imperial War Museum, Duxford Airfield, Cambridge CB2 4QR.**

PRELUDE

For most of recorded history, the south-east of Britain has been perceived as the part of the country most vulnerable to attack and invasion. It was in Kent that the Romans invaded and it was in this county that they found it necessary to build, at **Reculver**, **Richborough**, **Dover** and **Lympne**, four of the ten or eleven forts constructed to defend a stretch of coastline known as the 'Saxon Shore' because of the depredations of Saxon raiders.

About 750 years later, William of Normandy invaded at Pevensey, only a few miles from the Kent–Sussex border. It was in Kent that Henry VIII built the heaviest concentration of his coastal defence forts after the split from Rome: at **Sandown**, **Deal**, **Walmer** and **Sandgate**, with works added at Dover and the existing castle at Camber renovated and improved. In 1588, the southeast coast was threatened by the Spanish Armada and, in 1665–67, Kent was raided by the Dutch fleet to the despair of Samuel Pepys and his contemporaries. The proximity of the capital to Kent heightened an enduring sense of the county's vulnerability.

Napoleon Bonaparte's *Armée de l'Angleterre* camped on the French cliffs opposite Kent wanting 'only a favourable wind to plant the Imperial Eagle on the Tower of London'. Fear of renewed French aggression, stimulated by alarming advances in naval technology, was recurrent in late-nineteenth-century

Britain. Towards the end of the century, Germany emerged as a potential enemy and resources were diverted to the protection of the east coast. Even then, the defences of the south-east were considered vitally important.

War, when it came in 1914, brought many surprises. The threat from a modern and well-equipped German navy had long been recognised but now, for the first time, there were aircraft and airships to contend with as well. This lesson was forcefully brought home when German aircraft dropped bombs on Dover on Christmas Eve, 1914. War was no longer an activity conducted exclusively abroad by professional soldiers or Britain's foreign allies. The menace of aerial bombardment loomed over civilian and serviceman alike.

In 1940, when invasion seemed imminent after the fall of France, the defence of Kent was once again given high priority. Later in the war, Dover suffered extensively from shells fired by long-range German guns on the French coast. When Hitler resorted to *Vergeltungswaffen* – weapons of revenge, the V-weapons – it was in Kent that most of the anti-V-1 (codenamed DIVER) guns were sited.

The advent of nuclear technology and the phenomenon of 'Cold War' brought a fresh wave of civil defence measures. Yet the threat of mass destruction hung over continents rather than counties and Kent could no longer claim to be alone in the front line of national defence.

During the 1960s and 1970s, Kent County Council, in common with several other councils, pursued a vigorous 'eyesore clearance' programme. Pillboxes, anti-aircraft batteries, coastal defence installations and many other obsolete military structures were destroyed with almost reckless abandon. Now, at last, there is a growing interest in the defences of the twentieth century and these sites are increasingly accorded archaeological significance.

There are some enduring lessons to be learnt from

the study of Kent's recent military past. The most sig-
nificant is that the historical value of defensive sites is
seldom realised until the last example faces destruction. With the rapid growth in public interest during
recent years, it is possible that the structures of the
Cold War period might fare better than their Second
World War predecessors. Just as yesterday's junk is
today's 'collectable' and will be tomorrow's antique,
so yesterday's 'eyesore' may now survive to become
tomorrow's listed building or scheduled monument.

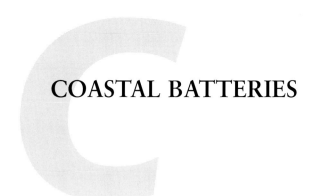

COASTAL BATTERIES

Coastal defence batteries number among the earliest military structures of the twentieth century in Britain. For hundreds of years, our coasts were defended by muzzle-loading guns similar to those deployed on ships. During the second half of the nineteenth century, rifled muzzle-loading guns were introduced and new batteries were built to emplace them. By the end of the century, reliable breech-loading guns with greatly improved muzzle velocity, range, accuracy and rate of fire had come into naval service. Such were the advantages of breech-loading guns aboard ship that it became imperative to arm coastal defence batteries with them as well. The alternative was to allow enemy warships an opportunity of bombarding obsolescent coastal installations with impunity.

Many of the coastal defence batteries built at the turn of the century remained in service throughout both world wars. New and improved guns were emplaced as they became available and an uneven process of modernisation continued until the abolition of coastal defence artillery in 1956. Sadly, few easily accessible batteries have survived in Kent: two that have are **Langdon Battery** at **Dover** and **New Tavern Fort** (Fort Gardens) at **Gravesend**.

At Langdon the battery was constructed for two 9.2-inch and three 6-inch guns, but the 9.2-inch emplacements are now occupied by a Coastguard station.

Opposite
Gun tower for No. 2 gun, also with observation post; Martello Battery, Sheerness

4.7-inch gun tower with later observation posts on top and behind; Martello Battery, Sheerness

At New Tavern Fort the battery was built on defences overlooking the River Thames. Commenced in 1778 and extensively remodelled during the nineteenth century, the battery once boasted two 6-inch guns. Both pieces have been replaced in recent years but the Fort now displays a collection of other guns and is a very pleasant spot in which to spend time on a sunny day.

Several coastal defence batteries are to be seen at **Sheerness** and at various points along the north coast of the Isle of Sheppey. **Martello Battery** at **Sheerness** is a particularly striking example of its kind with two 4.7-inch gun emplacements mounted on concrete towers and a later battery observation post disguised with a hipped roof. The battery is clearly visible from outside and to the east of the port area.

After Dunkirk, with invasion not only possible but probable, there was a rush to augment existing defences and arm the many undefended stretches of

coastline between heavily protected ports and dock-yards. The Navy had large numbers of 6-inch guns in store and these were used for 'emergency batteries'. The typical emergency battery had two 6-inch guns emplaced in concrete 'gun-houses' with overhead cover against aircraft attack. Good examples are to be seen at **Dover**, **Folkestone** and **Dymchurch**.

At Dover, **St Martin's Battery** on the Western Heights had acquired three 10-inch rifled muzzle-loading guns in the nineteenth century. In 1940, the unusual step was taken of building three gun-houses on top of the old battery, each with a 6-inch gun. The battery is easily accessible from the Western Heights roundabout on the A20. It is an interesting combination of nineteenth- and twentieth-century work, but the two periods are quite easily distinguished by the brickwork and concrete. If the bricks are muddy yellow they are nineteenth-century, if red they date from the twentieth century. Characteristically, nineteenth-century concrete is of rather coarser texture than that

A 6-inch emergency battery gun-house (and later additions); Dymchurch Redoubt

Above

A 6-inch emergency battery gun-house with holdfast for gun clearly visible. The wavy-topped wall is to break up the square shape of the gun-house as seen from the sea; St Martin's Battery, Dover

Right

Another 6-inch emergency battery gun-house; Copt Point Battery, Folkestone

of the twentieth century.

At **Folkestone**, a Second World War two-gun battery was built at Copt Point, close to Martello Tower No. 3. The gun-houses survive and one is now used for storage. The battery observation post may be seen above and behind the battery.

At **Dymchurch**, a two-gun battery was built, together with several machine-gun emplacements, on the nineteenth-century Grand Redoubt on the edge of Hythe Range. The Redoubt, unfortunately, is not accessible to the public but the battery can be seen from the beach and the battery observation post is a short distance to the west on the sea wall.

During the Second World War, several new coastal defence batteries were constructed to the north and south of Dover: Lydden Spout Battery (three 6-inch guns), Hougham Battery (three 8-inch), Fan Bay Battery (three 6-inch), South Foreland Battery (four 9.2-inch), and Wanstone Battery (two 15-inch). There were also two single 14-inch guns known as 'Winnie' and 'Pooh'.

These defences were augmented by three First World War 13.5-inch guns mounted on huge railway trucks. A former contractor's railway line from Martin Mill on the Dover–Deal line was partly relaid and extended to St Margaret's to serve 'Winnie', 'Pooh' and Wanstone Battery. Firing spurs were provided for the rail-mounted guns.

South Foreland Battery, between St Margaret's Road and Lighthouse Road at **St Margaret's at Cliffe**, may still be visited. The four gun positions can be seen, together with a magazine and the one representative barrack building that escaped 'eyesore clearance'. The railway can still be traced on the map and (less easily) on the ground. Of the other batteries little survives, but there are several observation posts on the cliff edge west of Dover which are clearly visible from the A20.

HARBOUR DEFENCES

Mainstay of harbour defence during the first part of the century was the 12pdr quick-firing (QF) gun designed for use against small craft such as torpedo-boats. During the Second World War, many 12pdr batteries were re-equipped with twin 6pdr guns (known as 'Twin Sixes') with a very much faster rate of fire. Such batteries, where they have survived, are seldom accessible but 12pdr emplacements may be seen at **Gravesend's New Tavern Fort**.

Targets for coastal and harbour defence batteries would be illuminated at night by searchlights, known as DELs (Defence Electric Lights) during the First World War and CASLs (Coast Artillery Searchlights) during the Second World War. Searchlight positions were built of steel or concrete and usually had a semicircular front with sliding shutters. Examples may be seen on the **Breakwater** at **Dover** and on the seaward side of the Dover–Folkestone railway line just outside Dover.

Ports and harbours were also frequently protected in

Opposite
A 12pdr gun in its emplacement; New Tavern Fort, Gravesend

Below
Coast Artillery Searchlight (CASL); Garrison Point Fort, Sheerness

both world wars by floating booms, or barriers, by anti-torpedo netting or by block ships sunk in harbour entrances. Few remains of such defences are now visible, but the hawse-holes for Dover's booms may be seen in the pier-heads at low tide. Just off **Grain**, on the **Isle of Grain**, is the nineteenth-century **Grain Tower** which can be visited at low tide. The tower was the anchorage for one end of a boom, the chain for which may still be seen at the tower's base. The tower also has emplacements for breech-loading guns and a position on its roof for a Second World War 6pdr in an anti-aircraft role. Remarkably, there is a Second World War barrack block on stilts beside it.

Another form of harbour defence was the electrically operated minefield under control of an XDO or EXDO (Extended Defence Officer). In many cases, the XDO used an existing building which offered a good view of the minefield. Alternatively, a purpose-built XDO post was constructed. Good examples of XDO posts survive on **Martello Tower No. 3** at **Folkestone's East Cliff** and at **Shell Ness** on the **Isle of Sheppey**.

Any vessel wishing to enter a harbour had to show a visual recognition signal, (flags by day or lights by night), or give a sound signal during times of poor visibility. These signals were usually changed daily and any vessel not showing the correct signal would be challenged by the Port War Signal Station. If necessary, suspect vessels were stopped by a 'bring to' round fired across the bows from a designated 'examination battery'. The vessel would then be directed to an anchorage or mooring under the guns of the examination battery where she would be boarded and her intentions ascertained. The Port War Signal Station at **Dover** still remains on the edge of the cliff in front of the Castle.

Certainly the most remarkable of harbour defences was the Brennan torpedo which was adopted in 1887 and remained in service until 1903, just about long enough to qualify as a twentieth-century

Brennan torpedo opera-
tor's conning position;
Garrison Point Fort,
Sheerness

defence. Louis Brennan, an Irish Australian, was a
prolific inventor but his torpedo was surely his most
inspired creation. The device was launched from the
land and carried two drums of wire. The wire was
extracted from its rear by a steam-driven shore-based
winch. The drums were connected to contra-rotating
propellers, and a steering lever in the torpedo operator's conning position allowed the rate at which the
wires were recovered to be varied. A differential gear
in the torpedo permitted control of the rudder.

Brennan torpedo stations were built at the nineteenth-century **Garrison Point Fort** at Sheerness,
and at **Cliffe Fort** on the **Hoo peninsula**. Garrison
Point Fort was the Brennan torpedo 'school' and has
the remains of three conning positions. The launching rails can be seen at low tide.

At Cliffe, a retractable observation/conning tower
was built and launching rails survive. Unfortunately,
neither fort is easily accessible. Garrison Point is

13

Position for Brennan torpedo operator's retractable conning tower; Cliffe Fort

inside Sheerness docks while Cliffe Fort is remotely situated on privately-owned land.

The Brennan torpedo was withdrawn from service in 1903 after the emplacement of reliable breech-loading guns for the defence of harbours and navigable rivers. Breech-loaders, with their longer range, increased accuracy and far more rapid rate of fire than the cumbersome rifled muzzle-loading guns which they replaced, had made the Brennan torpedo unnecessary. The Royal Engineers' Museum at **Gillingham** contains the sole surviving example of this, the world's first guided weapon.

ACTIVE AIR DEFENCE

When enemy aircraft and airships first began to drop bombs on Britain in the First World War, there was no organised air defence system and any available guns were used to try to shoot them down. These efforts were usually unsuccessful. Purpose-built anti-aircraft (AA) batteries usually mounted quite small guns although a 6-inch naval gun, mounted on a railway truck, is known to have been used on the **Prince of Wales's Pier** at **Dover**. Very few First World War AA batteries have survived in recognisable form.

Between the wars, anti-aircraft technology was improved to incorporate the lessons of the First World War. First into service were 3-inch guns followed by 3.7-inch, 4.5-inch and 5.25-inch guns. Smaller guns such as the Oerlikon and 40mm Bofors were mounted wherever attacks by low-flying aircraft seemed likely.

Heavy AA batteries, which mounted the larger guns, may be seen at several places in Kent. Good examples are on the seaward side of the Dover to St Margaret's

Heavy AA battery, gun store; Farthingloe, Dover

Above
Heavy AA battery, gun emplacement showing ammunition lockers and gun holdfast; Farthingloe, Dover

Right
Heavy AA battery, five-bay magazine; Farthingloe, Dover

coast road just east of **Sherley's Farm** (which itself includes a 5.25-inch AA battery); on the **Western Heights** on the Folkestone side of Dover; and on the north side of **Wallhouse Road** in **Erith**. Another can be seen from the M2 motorway in a field on the north side of the motorway between the A251 and A249 junctions. Most heavy AA batteries consist of four gun emplacements laid out in a semicircle with the battery's command post at the centre.

Mention should also be made of the offshore forts in the **Thames Estuary**, designed by the civil engineer G A Maunsell. These were of two types, one designed for Navy use, the other for Army use. The four Navy forts resembled large rafts on legs and mounted two 3.7-inch and two 40mm Bofors AA guns. The three Army forts consisted of groups of seven steel boxes on stilts, connected by catwalks. One tower carried a searchlight, one was armed with Bofors guns, one acted as control tower and the other four towers each had one 3.7-inch gun. Abandoned after the Second World War, all the forts

A 3.7-inch AA gun from the Tongue Sands offshore fort; New Tavern Fort, Gravesend

were used at one time or another by pirate radio stations. Two surviving Army forts can be seen from the north Kent coast on clear days. A 3.7-inch AA gun from a Navy fort is displayed at **New Tavern Fort** at **Gravesend**.

Later in the Second World War, when V-1 flying bombs became a menace, huge numbers of AA guns were moved to north Kent and then to the coast. The guns were emplaced on temporary platforms made up of lengths of railway line and known as 'Pile Mattresses' after General Sir Frederick Pile, the General Officer Commanding AA Command. DIVER batteries, as they were known, were quite short-lived and rarely associated with permanent buildings. Today, there are few reminders of their existence apart from occasional crop marks.

Light AA sites were equally insubstantial since the guns were usually surrounded by simple earthworks

Type 22 pillbox with light AA emplacement on roof; Swingate, Dover

Above
Type 24 pillbox with light
AA emplacement on roof;
Hawkinge

Left
Detail of AA gun
mounting; Hawkinge

Bofors AA tower;
Dunkirk

or protective walls of concrete blocks and sandbags. Most have disappeared without trace. In parts of Kent, pillboxes survive with light AA emplacements on their roofs. A particularly good example may be seen at **Hawkinge**, beside the minor road which runs along the south-west side of the airfield. At **Dunkirk**, west of **Canterbury**, is a rare Bofors tower, a substantial concrete construction which stands in a wood to the west of the former Chain Home radar station. The 6pdr AA emplacement on **Grain Tower** has already been mentioned.

Yet another AA defence which has left few traces is the 'Z' battery. These units fired 3-inch rockets and required few if any permanent constructions.

Searchlight sites consisted of a circular earthwork about 30ft in diameter for the searchlight itself. There was also an emplacement for the predictor, a light AA gun pit, and huts for generator and crew. Most have survived only as crop marks but occasionally surviving huts or their foundations may be found.

PASSIVE
AIR DEFENCE

After the First World War, far more attention was given to defence against airborne attack. It was realised that a good deal of the trouble in dealing with enemy aircraft was that, once an aircraft had been heard, seen and identified, it was usually too late to catch it, let alone shoot it down. Clearly, some means of early warning of an enemy aircraft's approach was needed.

Early experiments in long-range acoustic detection of aircraft were carried out in 1918 and in the 1920s the first sound mirrors were built, acting with sound in much the same way as a concave mirror acts with light. An operator stood in front of the mirror with a stethoscope. When the sound of an aircraft was picked up, the operator would move the stethoscope's trumpet-shaped 'business end', known as the sound collector, about the mirror until the sound was strongest, so getting a reasonably accurate bearing on the intruder. If bearings were taken from two or three mirrors, separated by a few miles, and their point of intersection plotted, quite an accurate fix could be obtained.

The earliest acoustic device was the slab mirror, a monolithic concrete construction with a 20ft diameter concave dish in the front. Next came 30ft diameter hemispherical bowl mirrors and finally a 200ft curved wall mirror with a series of microphones along its forecourt. The bowl mirror operator, instead of

standing on a platform in front of the mirror, sat in a small room underneath it and worked the sound collector by remote control. For the 200ft wall mirror, a control room was built behind the mirror and the operator listened to each microphone in turn.

Under ideal conditions, sound mirrors worked well, detecting aircraft at ranges of up to 20 miles. Unfortunately, however, climatic conditions were often far from ideal in Kent and with high winds the mirrors' performance declined markedly. They were also adversely affected by extraneous noises. Traffic on nearby roads, waves crashing on to a beach or even a passing ship could mask the sound of an aircraft. Difficulties were compounded by the relentless advance of aviation technology and the shorter warning time afforded by faster aircraft. With an aircraft flying at 60mph, detection at a range of 20 miles meant 20 minutes warning. Once aircraft were flying at 300mph, detection at the same range meant only four minutes' warning. What was needed was some means of detecting aircraft reliably at long

Above
Denge 200ft wall mirror;
Romney Marsh

Opposite
Denge slab mirror;
Romney Marsh

Bowl mirror from rear;
Hythe

range.

The answer, of course, was radar and it was this which, during the Battle of Britain, allowed the RAF to dispatch fighter aircraft from airfields in Kent and elsewhere to meet enemy aircraft. The sound mirrors were finally abandoned in 1939 but there is a persistent rumour that they were briefly reactivated in 1940 when it was feared that the Germans might have found some way of jamming radar.

South of **Greatstone,** in the vicinity of **Denge** and **Dungeness**, is a remarkable group of acoustic devices comprising a slab mirror, a bowl mirror and Britain's only 200ft wall mirror. They are on private land but may be seen from the coast road. A bowl mirror can be inspected at close quarters on the hill above **Hythe** on an area known as '**The Roughs**'. A slab mirror close by has fallen flat on its face because of the unstable ground here but an upright example can be seen at **Abbot's Cliff**, east of **Capel**.

Slab mirrors at **Fan Bay**, just north of **Dover**, were buried during Kent County Council's 'eyesore clear-

Above
Slab sound mirror;
Abbot's Cliff, near Capel

Left
Frontal view of Abbot's
Cliff mirror

Opposite Above
Chain Home radar Rx
control block; Swingate,
Dover

Opposite Below
Chain Home radar, con-
crete bases of wooden Rx
tower; Swingate, Dover

ance' programme and another at **Warden Point** on the **Isle of Sheppey** has succumbed to coast erosion. More isolated mirrors exist further north on the east coast. The Greatstone, Hythe and Abbot's Cliff mirrors are particularly important examples since they were always intended to operate together as a discrete system.

Radar was developed from 1935 onwards at **Orford Ness** and later at **Bawdsey** in Suffolk. The earliest service stations were given the nomenclature 'Chain Home'. Chain Home sites were characterised by four transmitting (Tx) aerials on 350ft steel towers and four receiving (Rx) aerials on 240ft timber towers. Other buildings included the Tx and Rx control blocks – heavily blast-proofed by surrounding earthen banks and with a 5ft 6in layer of shingle in the roof to help absorb the impact of a direct hit – a stand-by generator in case of power failure and a guardroom with accommodation huts. Each site also had its own defences comprising trenches, pillboxes and often light anti-aircraft weapons. Partially surviving Chain Home stations are at **Swingate**, just north of **Dover**, and **Dunkirk**, west of **Canterbury**. At Swingate, two Tx towers survive, together with one replacement tower. At Dunkirk, one Tx tower remains.

Later radar installations, known as Chain Home Low, were originally designed to improve detection of low-flying aircraft. Coast Defence/Chain Home Low provided radar plotting of both aircraft and shipping while Chain Home Extra Low gave much improved sea-level coverage. These sites are far less substantial than the Chain Home stations and few, if any, remain in Kent.

While radar could provide early warning, it was some time before friendly aircraft could be distinguished from those of the enemy. This was the task of the Observer Corps. The Corps was formed in 1925 as a result of air defence exercises conducted in 1924 and centred on **Cranbrook** in Kent. The 'Royal'

prefix was awarded during the Second World War in recognition of its services. The Corps' first members were enrolled as special constables and by 1938 there was a network of observation posts covering most of southern and eastern England.

Early Observer Corps posts were very temporary affairs, often no more than a piece of corrugated iron supported on bales of straw as some protection from the elements. Early in the Second World War, wooden huts were provided but some post crews, particularly those with connections in the building trade, had already provided themselves with some rather more permanent shelter. Such shelters have seldom survived but one remains at **Ham Street** on the B2067.

Another commonplace of wartime Britain was the barrage balloon. The purpose of these balloons was to force enemy aircraft to fly higher and so make accurate bombing more difficult. During the V-1 period, a belt of barrage balloons acted as a 'long stop' south of London in the hope that any V-1s which evaded the coastal anti-aircraft batteries or inland fighter patrols would foul the balloon cables and crash. Barrage balloon sites were insubstantial and it is unlikely that there will be any remains apart from isolated balloon mooring rings.

Decoy sites existed for all important airfields in the hope that they, and not the airfields, would be bombed. The Luftwaffe, however, were not easily fooled and most daylight airfield decoys were abandoned by 1941. Night-time decoys were rather more successful, with exposed lights to attract bombers and sudden fires to simulate successful bombing. Decoys tended to cover large areas of land, with few permanent buildings, and little is likely to have survived apart from the control shelters. Scant remains of the decoy for **Sheerness Docks** are known to exist on **Graveney Marshes**.

ANTI-INVASION DEFENCES

The ubiquitous pillbox is, of course, the best-known anti-invasion defence. These unlovely structures remain a commonplace throughout Kent in hedgerows, allotments, back gardens and even inside already existing buildings. The popular assumption that they were built haphazardly to a single design is entirely misplaced.

Pillboxes were carefully sited to defend vulnerable beaches, airfields, coastal defence batteries, level crossings, important road junctions, radar stations and factories. More importantly, they were used, in conjunction with other defences, to form stop lines and to harden the coastal crust. Good examples of stop lines are the Corps Line, which follows the Dover–Canterbury railway north-north-west from **Shepherdswell**, and a short line which runs round the east side of **Hoo St Werburgh** from the A228 to the **River Medway**. The most important stop line, however, was the GHQ Line which runs from east of **London** down to the **Sevenoaks** area and then west into Surrey and beyond. A good coastal crust line of pillboxes can be seen along the top of the escarpment which overlooks **Folkestone**.

Second World War pillboxes generally conform to drawings prepared by branch FW3 of the War Office's Directorate of Fortifications and Works and are usually known by their drawing numbers – FW3/22, FW3/23 and so on – or, more familiarly, as

Above
Type 23 pillbox with
crenel (which also forms
entrance) in open section;
Citadel Battery, Dover

Right
Type 22 pillbox overlook-
ing Folkestone

Type 23 pillbox; St
Martin's Battery, Dover

the Type 22, Type 23 etc. The most common pillbox designs are as follows:

Type 22 – regular hexagon with walls approximately 6ft long; designed for infantry with rifles and light machine-guns

Type 23 – rectangular with a roofed section approximately 8ft by 8ft and an open section the same size for a light AA weapon

Type 24 – hexagonal but with a rear wall approximately 14ft long and adjoining walls which meet it at an angle of about 90 degrees; designed for infantry with light machine-guns

Type 25 – circular, otherwise as for Type 22

Type 26 – square, approximately 8ft by 8ft, otherwise as for Type 22

Type 27 – large hexagon or octagon with an open area in the centre for a light AA weapon

Type 28 – large and rectangular with thick walls; designed for 2pdr or 6pdr anti-tank gun

Right
Type 24 pillbox;
Bekesbourne

Below
Type 24 pillbox.
Sometimes they're not so
easy to find; Poison Cross,
near Eastry

Above
Light machine-gun 'tables'
in Type 24 pillbox;
Folkestone

Left
Type 28 pillbox, embra-
sure; Adisham

Above
Holdfast inside embrasure
for 6pdr anti-tank gun;
Adisham

Opposite Above
Non-standard square pill-
box; Dover

Opposite Below
Anti-tank gun pillbox;
behind Dover Castle

Type 28a – as for Type 28 but with a separate chamber for infantry

Type 28a Twin – as for Type 28a but with two anti-tank gun embrasures in two adjoining walls.

A thick-walled version of the Type 24 is sometimes referred to as a Type 29 but this is not an official 'Type' number and is not used in this series.

There were other standard types, often with specialised functions, which deserve mention although they are rarely found in Kent. The Norcon was little more than a short length of 6ft-diameter concrete pipe set upright with embrasures cut in it. The Alan Williams turret took the form of a domed steel roof mounted over a pit while the Pickett-Hamilton retractable fort spent most of its active life underground. The latter structure was intended for airfield protection and could be raised hydraulically when local defence became a more pressing consideration than aircraft safety. A modern variant of the Norcon is the Yarnold Sanger which may sometimes be seen at or near the entrances to military establishments.

Pillbox built into garage; Court-at-Street

In addition to the standard types, there were many non-standard pillboxes, often built to suit a particular location. At **Adisham**, two small rectangular pillboxes are built into a railway bridge while at **Dover** there are many non-standard square pillboxes on the hills above the town (so many, in fact, as almost to form a 'Type' of their own). **Dover Castle** has a small 6pdr gun pillbox built into its wall near Constable's Gate and **Aylesford** has a 6pdr gun pillbox concealed in a garage. Another garage converted into a pillbox stands in **Court-at-Street** on the B2067. In some cases, a house had a room reinforced and effectively turned into a pillbox. One example is known to have existed in Dover. There were at least two more in **Ashford** and several others were in the Medway towns.

Pillboxes are almost invariably of reinforced con-

Above

Field-gun emplacement, heavily overgrown; The Danes recreation ground, Dover

Left

Field-gun emplacement of concrete-filled bags; Elms Vale, Dover

Field-gun emplacement with 'mini' pillbox alongside and downhill; Citadel Battery, Dover.

crete, shuttered with whatever material was most conveniently to hand. Wood was the most commonly used shuttering material and the rough-sawn planks often left a visible imprint in the concrete. Corrugated iron was sometimes used, particularly inside pillboxes for the underside of the roof, and many pillboxes used brick shuttering which was left in place after the concrete had set. This sometimes gives the misleading appearance of a brick-built structure.

It must be remembered that not all pillboxes date from the Second World War. There were fears of invasion early in the First World War as well, and some pillboxes date from this period. Known examples are a circular pillbox on **Fort Burgoyne** at Dover, visible from the lay-by on the minor road from Dover to **Guston**, and a small square pillbox on the north side of the A249 Maidstone to Sheppey road close to the junction with the M2. Other reminders of the 1914–18 war survive along the top of the hill to the north of the Maidstone to M2 stretch of the A249. This piece of high ground also features some the First

World War earthwork remains from what was known as the Chatham Land Front.

The sheer physical effort involved in pillbox construction should not be underestimated. All the concrete used had to be transported to the site as cement, sand, aggregate and water, and then mixed on the spot. A little simple arithmetic will show that, since a cubic yard of concrete weighs roughly a ton, even a Type 22 pillbox, which is not particularly big or thick-walled, demanded something like 20 tons of concrete with additional steel reinforcement.

A pillbox in the front garden can make a good conversation piece, too

Type 24 with 'beefed up' front walls; Walmer

In addition to the Type 28 pillbox, a number of field-gun emplacements and other purpose-built anti-tank gun emplacements survive. Fort Burgoyne at Dover has no less than seven concrete field-gun emplacements and another is on the edge of a recreation ground known as **The Danes** half a mile or so west.

Anti-tank blocks were made in colossal quantities and came in a number of standard forms. The most common varieties were cubes with sides of 3ft 6in or 5ft, 'pimples' or dragon's teeth like flat-topped pyramids, 'coffins' measuring 5ft long, 3ft wide and 3ft high, and cylinders 3ft high and 2ft in diameter. Lengths of railway line bent into a 'U' or 'V' shape and slotted into sockets in roads were also found to be effective. Anti-tank blocks and rails were usually placed in multiple rows. Good examples may be seen at **Dover Castle**, where they were intended to close

Above
Disguised emplacement
for 6pdr anti-tank gun;
Kingsdown

Left
Mounting beside road for
6pdr anti-tank gun;
Snowdown

Pillbox just visible in
right-hand arch of bridge;
Adisham

off one end of an anti-tank ditch (they are covered by
the 6pdr gun pillbox in the wall referred to above).
Further specimens are in **Court-at-Street** on the
B2067, on the western edge of the **Port Lympne
Wildlife Park**, and at **Graveney Marshes**, close to
the shore just off the minor road to the west of
Whitstable.

In addition to anti-tank blocks, an excellent example of an anti-tank wall survives at **Walmer** just to
the south of **Walmer Castle**. Here, a house has its
front garden wall 'beefed up' with 3ft or so of concrete, and on the other side of the unmade road
which adjoins the house there is an anti-tank fence
comprising lengths of railway line and I-section steel
girders in the hedgerow.

Many lengths of anti-tank ditch were dug, usually

THE
DEFENCE

OF
BRITAIN

planned to incorporate 'ready-made' features such as rivers, canals and railway cuttings. These features were usually backed by pillboxes and anti-tank gun emplacements. All were filled in late in the Second World War or shortly afterwards and the anti-tank ditch typically survives only as a shallow nondescript depression or as a strip of contrasting colour across a newly-ploughed field. An excellent example of a 'ready-made' anti-tank ditch is the **Royal Military Canal**, originally cut to impede an invading French army in the nineteenth century. Several pillboxes endure along its length.

Another form of anti-invasion defence, the road block, came in several forms. Obsolete farm equipment stood ready to be dragged across many rural roads. Gates could be dropped into slots on concrete blocks or concrete cones might be lifted into position on the road itself. The obsolete farm equipment and gates have long gone but you can often see the concrete cones at the sides of country roads, especially at junctions, still waiting for the invasion that never came. Three rows of the sockets into which they would have fitted may be seen on a railway bridge on

Machine-gun post;
Dymchurch Redoubt

the minor road from **Barfrestone** to **Woolage Village**.

None of the obstacles mentioned here was seriously intended to destroy vehicles, let alone a tank. Their purpose was to slow or channel an enemy advance so that weapons could be brought to bear more effectively. It is always interesting, therefore, to examine the ground surrounding road block sites in order to determine the likely location of minefields or weapons that could give covering fire.

One such weapon was the spigot mortar or Blacker Bombard. This ungainly device had a range of around 400yds and was intended as an anti-tank or anti-personnel weapon. Its emplacement was a pit with a domed concrete 'thimble' at its centre. On the top of the 'thimble' was a stainless steel pin on which the mortar was mounted. Spigot mortar mountings are to be found throughout the county, often near coastal defence batteries, radar stations, bridges and important road junctions. They have seldom been moved from their original positions but the pits are usually filled in and the mounting, only a little above

Opposite Above
Anti-tank cubes; Graveney Marshes

Opposite Below
Anti-tank cubes, showing foundation raft; Bekesbourne

Below
Spigot mortar mounting; Citadel Battery, Dover

ground level, is often inconspicuous or overgrown.

Among the nastier defensive weapons of the Second World War were the flame devices. One of these was the flame fougasse which, in its simplest form, was a 40-gallon drum filled with a mixture of petrol, oil and rubber and fitted with an explosive charge. Variations were the 'hedge hopper' – which could jump 10ft vertically and travel 30ft horizontally before engulfing anything below it in flames – and the 'cliff hopper' which could jump off a cliff top with much the same result for those below.

More substantial installations were the 'burning beach' and 'sea flame barrage', both of which used fixed pipes to deliver fuel on to a likely invasion beach or into the sea just below low-water mark. Such systems were either gravity-fed or used a pump to push the fuel to its destination. An installation at Dover, removed only recently for the new A20, had a pump house and three fuel tanks, each approximately 20ft long and 8ft in diameter. The pipework of such systems may occasionally be seen on beaches when exposed by storms.

Anti-tank pimples at edge of wood, Court-at-Street, still waiting for the invasion that never came. Summer is not the best time to look for them!

Road block sockets;
Barfrestone to Woolage
Village road

Particularly vulnerable beaches were often mined and defended with lengths of scaffolding or barbed wire. Pillboxes and reinforced-concrete gun-houses were commonplace, designed to allow guns to fire from both sides down the length of a beach. Most of these defences were removed long ago but their remains, like those of the petroleum warfare installations, sometimes emerge after heavy weather.

It would be wrong to describe the archaeology of Kent's wartime defences without mention of the Home Guard and Auxiliary Units. The popular television series *Dad's Army* concentrated on the amateur nature of the Home Guard for the sake of comedy, portraying its members as juveniles and geriatrics. Nevertheless, the importance of the Home Guard in the event of invasion would be difficult to overstate. Even after the threat of invasion had passed and

Above
Vickers heavy machine-gun pillbox GHQ Line beside A26, guarding the Maidstone to Paddock Wood railway line and River Medway; Teston, west of Maidstone

Right
Type 24 of GHQ Line, as seen from the Vickers heavy machine-gun pill-box at Teston, west of Maidstone

plans were being drawn up for the Allied invasion of Europe, the Home Guard, by taking over many coastal defence and anti-aircraft batteries, released for the offensive many men who would otherwise have been engaged on more mundane duties. Churchill himself recognised the significance of the Home Guard for civilian morale. Today, the only surviving structures which have definite Home Guard connections are brick-built equipment stores. These buildings typically have flat concrete roofs with two slit windows at one end and a door at the other. None are known to exist in Kent.

'Auxiliary Unit' was the wonderfully innocuous name given to groups of men trained in demolition and sabotage techniques so that they could form the nucleus of a British resistance movement. Gamekeepers and poachers were frequently chosen as 'Patrol Leaders', since they knew the countryside best, and they selected their own men from their own communities. Each patrol was provided with an operational base, always very well hidden and usually underground. All of these bases were supposed to have been destroyed by Royal Engineers demolition squads after the war but some have survived because the Engineers simply failed to find them. For further information on Auxiliary Units, David Lampe's book *The Last Ditch* is recommended (see bibliography).

AIRFIELDS

Military aviation, using balloons, began in Britain in 1878 at **Woolwich Arsenal** and the first military aerodrome was built at **Larkhill** on **Salisbury Plain** in 1911. Meanwhile, in Kent, a site at **Eastchurch** on the **Isle of Sheppey** (now an open prison) was leased to the Royal Aero Club in 1910 and quickly became a base for such aviation pioneers as Moore-Brabazon, Rolls, Sopwith and the Short brothers. The first of many Royal Navy personnel arrived at Eastchurch to train as pilots in April 1911. By the end of the First World War, Kent had about 20 aerodromes, airship and seaplane bases.

Early airfields needed no more than a fairly level grass field with a few hangars for aircraft and huts for accommodation, administration and storage. None of those in Kent has survived in anything like a complete state but the former airfield at **Bekesbourne** still has a First World War Belfast truss hangar. The Belfast truss, first manufactured by Anderson & Co of Belfast, was a lattice of interwoven pine slats which could be assembled by unskilled labour to provide wide-span roof supports. Some specialists believe that the idea was originally copied from German indoor riding schools.

Many airfields were returned to agriculture shortly after the First World War and were not revived during the Second World War because they were by

Opposite
First World War Belfast truss hangar; Bekesbourne

First World War adminis-
tration buildings; Dover
(Marine Parade) seaplane
base

then too small. Even where airfields remained in service or were reused, **Biggin Hill** for example, the majority of First World War buildings were often replaced. The process of architectural attrition continues. Only a few years ago, the remaining airship hanger base at **Capel** vanished and it appears that the sole surviving administration building of the **Dover (Marine Parade)** seaplane base is to be sold for redevelopment.

In the wave of revulsion and disillusionment which followed the First World War, the Royal Air Force, born in 1918 from amalgamation of the Royal Flying Corps and the Royal Naval Air Service, suffered intense financial stringency. The Great War had been officially proclaimed as 'the war to end wars' and few were keen to spend money unnecessarily on the armed forces. By 1924, only 27 military aerodromes remained in the whole country and it was not until

the late 1920s, in response to fears of French competition, that a co-ordinated reconstruction programme began. The growth of Nazi Germany encouraged a further appraisal of defence needs and stimulated the RAF's Expansion Period.

Airfield buildings of the Expansion Period were of a very high standard, with accommodation buildings of neo-Georgian style, designs that were approved by

Left
Expansion Period officers' mess; RAF Hawkinge

Below
Expansion Period guard room; RAF West Malling

Above
Surface air-raid shelter;
Reinden Wood dispersed
site, RAF Hawkinge

Right
Entrance to blast shelter;
Reinden Wood dispersed
site, RAF Hawkinge

Opposite Above
Interior of blast shelter;
Reinden Wood dispersed
site, RAF Hawkinge

Opposite Below
Gas decontamination
building; Reinden Wood
dispersed site, RAF
54   Hawkinge

Gas decontamination
building; RAF Manston

the Royal Fine Arts Commission. The typical Expansion Period airfield had its buildings in a conveniently compact group but this was soon recognised as a mistake. After the first destructive months of the Battle of Britain, during which airfields were sometimes bombed twice or more in a day, a policy of dispersal was implemented. Administration and storage huts were scattered around the perimeter of airfields and the accommodation or 'domestic' sites were typically moved a mile or more away. Aircraft were also widely dispersed which, whilst less convenient for the aircrew, greatly increased their prospects of survival.

Airfield buildings of the Second World War were usually built hastily and were frequently characterised by a rough-and-ready appearance rather than any architectural merit. Many survive on airfields around the county but their numbers are slowly and steadily dwindling. Wartime airfields often have a museum at which it is possible to buy an official airfield plan showing former wartime buildings. These plans sometimes give Air Ministry specification numbers as well. Those interested in finding and identifying

Left
Top of Pickett-Hamilton retractable fort, *ex situ*; Hawkinge

Below
Airfield battle headquarters to Air Ministry design 11008/41

Above
Expansion Period work-
shops; RAF West Malling

Right
Control tower and J type
hangar; RAF West
Malling

wartime airfield buildings cannot do better than purchase *British Airfield Buildings of the Second World War* by Graham Buchan Innes (see bibliography).

All airfields needed defence against enemy aircraft and against possible attack by paratroops or invading infantry. Most of these defences are very similar, if not identical, to their anti-invasion, light anti-aircraft and civil defence counterparts. Two structures which are unique to airfields are the Pickett-Hamilton retractable fort, which has already been mentioned briefly, and the battle headquarters. The battle headquarters was intended to be manned only during an attack on the airfield and was usually positioned on the highest ground available for good visibility. The most common is that constructed to Air Ministry specification 11008/41, built of reinforced concrete and with a complex of five underground rooms. A command post, with a domed square observation cupola, protruded 3ft or so above the ground and gave a 360 degree field of view.

Below
Airfield huts; RAF Lympne

Detail
Detail of hut at Lympne, showing almost infallible clue to wartime construction: bricks laid on edge

CIVIL DEFENCE

Civil defence in the First World War was practically non-existent and civilians were left to find what shelter they could. The Air Raid Precautions (ARP) Act of 1937 placed a statutory obligation on local authorities to provide shelters and anti-gas precautions. The 1938 Munich Crisis gave an added urgency to such provision.

The most common domestic shelter of the Second World War was the corrugated iron Anderson shelter, hundreds of which are still in use as garden or allotment sheds. Public shelters were of many kinds, the simplest being a trench dug in a public space. Many shops and public buildings had their basements reinforced which were then designated as shelters. In Dover and elsewhere, existing chalk caves were extended and strengthened with concrete where necessary. In **Ramsgate**, a whole new system of concrete-lined tunnels was cut under the town to serve as

Opposite
ARP wardens' post; Priory Station, Dover

Below
Bricked-up entrance to chalk cave shelter; Dover

shelters. This was the more remarkable because work was begun as early as 1936.

Many schools were provided with shelters underneath their playgrounds. Surface shelters, strong brick and/or concrete constructions with blast-protected entrances, were also built. They gave protection only against blast and falling masonry or shell splinters. Rather more effective were semi-sunken shelters where earth was banked against walls and over roofs. These were often built of prefabricated concrete panels and were common on airfields or their dispersed 'domestic' sites.

Most underground shelters have been filled in or at least had their entrances blocked. Any unexplained blocked entrance in a wall with an earth or chalk bank behind it may be an entrance to a former shelter, particularly if it is beneath the playground of a school which fronts on to a road. Alternatively, it may be the entrance to a disused public lavatory! Two well-preserved surface shelters may be found in **Wallhouse Road**, leading on to **Erith Marshes**, and there are many more surface and semi-sunken shelters on airfields and their dispersed sites.

ARP centres were the kingpins of civilian air raid precautions. Their role was to receive reports from police, fire-watchers and wardens' posts and to co-ordinate rescue and fire services. Although ARP centres were usually situated in the basements of existing buildings (Town Halls and police stations were popular choices), there were also purpose-built structures.

ARP wardens' posts and first aid posts might also be located in existing buildings but many were purpose-built structures erected on convenient sites. Some have been converted since the Second World War into small workshops or offices but most have now been redeveloped. Good local knowledge or considerable research may be necessary to identify the sites of ARP centres, wardens' posts and first aid posts.

Opposite
The end of an underground air-raid shelter; Dover, 1996

THE DEFENCE
OF BRITAIN

Right
Air-raid siren; Buckland,
Dover

Below
Stanton semi-sunken air-
raid shelter. The 'chimney'
is the emergency exit;
Reinden Wood dispersed
site, RAF Hawkinge

Air-raid sirens were situated on the roofs of Town Halls, fire stations, police stations, wardens' posts and other public buildings. Each was reckoned to have an audible range of about one mile and all are now believed to have gone.

Gas decontamination centres were sometimes in requisitioned buildings but purpose-built structures were often provided. Minimum requirements were an undressing room, showers, drying and dressing rooms, and a furnace for disposing of contaminated clothing.

Some ARP maps and drawings have now found their way into local museums and libraries and can be useful sources of information. The writer was surprised to find from such a drawing that a building (now demolished) that he had known only as a dairy was originally built as a base for the local ARP rescue unit.

THE COLD WAR

Fast jet aircraft created much the same problems for radar as fast piston-engined aircraft had posed for the sound mirrors. Intruding aircraft had to be detected earlier and at longer range if the warnings were to be sufficient for interception.

The ROTOR programme, drawn up in 1949, used existing Chain Home radar cover for long-range detection and improved radar for low-level cover. Nuclear weapons were an obvious threat to existing radar stations and their personnel so ROTOR installations were, whenever possible, sited underground with only aerial arrays on the surface. The entrance to the underground structure was a standard guardhouse resembling a bungalow with a verandah supported on brick columns. Some are now in use as private residences. The main recognition points for a ROTOR guardhouse are the characteristic verandah and circular windows high up in the gabled ends of the building.

From the mid-1950s, the Type 80 radar, installed in ground-controlled interception stations, had a longer range than that of the ROTOR reporting stations. An obvious improvement was to combine the two functions in a single Master Station which integrated detection and interception. With a handful of Master Stations able to operate more efficiently than a whole chain of reporting stations, the ROTOR programme became obsolete.

Opposite
Royal Observer Corps
underground monitoring
post

With the advent of intercontinental ballistic missiles, coastal defence and anti-aircraft batteries were recognised as useless and dismantled. Official confidence was placed in the concept of deterrence based upon a clear and credible threat of retaliation to aggression. The North Atlantic Treaty Organisation, of which Britain became a founder member in 1949, envisaged a flexible military response in which the level of retaliation was determined by the level of aggression. This policy did not preclude the first use of nuclear weapons against an enemy, although the precise extent of provocation needed for such action was never clearly defined. The essence of deterrence might thus be described as uncertainty about the consequence of any hostile act. Potential antagonists lived under the shadow of Mutually Assured Destruction which ensured, if not peace, at least an absence of war between nuclear powers.

If deterrence had failed, the government of the country and the heads of its armed forces needed to be deep underground in order to conduct hostilities and try to manage their aftermath. Huge self-contained underground shelters were constructed and some were adapted from the ROTOR programme described earlier. Several local authorities constructed smaller versions for themselves but it is only within the last few years – with the emergence of a 'New World Order' – that some of these Regional and Sub-Regional Seats of Government are being acknowledged. A few have even been sold into private ownership.

The Royal Observer Corps was reformed in 1947 and maintained its role of aircraft reporting into the mid-1950s. The standard ROC post of the 1950s was the Orlit, named after the company (Orlit Ltd) which produced them.

The Orlit post came in two varieties. The Type A stood at ground level or was erected on top of an existing building, while the Type B rested on 4ft 6in concrete legs. In appearance the Orlit post is similar

to a large prefabricated concrete coal-bunker with an open observation section and a small roofed store/shelter with a wooden door. Access to the Type B was by a metal ladder. An Orlit post survives at **Brookland**, near **Lydd**, on a minor road south-south-west of the church.

From the mid-1950s onwards, the role of the ROC

Royal Observer Corps Orlit post; Brookland

was changed from aircraft observation to the monitoring of nuclear explosions and radioactive fallout. Thenceforward, the standard ROC post was a small reinforced-concrete underground monitoring bunker. The underground monitoring post had accommodation for three observers complete with bunks and a chemical closet in a small adjoining room. Access was by vertical steel ladder from a hatch in a small entrance stack which incorporated a ventilation shaft for the chemical closet. Many posts were abandoned in 1968 and the ROC was finally stood down in 1991.

The underground monitoring post is one of the more difficult twentieth-century defences to find. All that shows above ground is the concrete entrance, approximately 3ft high and 3ft square, a metal pipe with a flange on to which the fixed survey meter probe was bolted, a small pipe for the bomb power indicator baffle-plate, and the 3ft high 1ft square ventilator stack. Each post was in a small compound surrounded by chain-link fence but, particularly in the case of posts abandoned in 1968, the fence is often long gone. Most posts are sited unobtrusively beside minor roads but some are next to main highways. Clues which suggest an underground monitoring post include a small lay-by for crew members' cars or a gateway in a hedgerow. Sometimes, the only indication is a glimpse of chain-link fence behind a hedge or steps leading apparently nowhere up a bank at the side of the road. Easily found examples are at **Brookland**, next to the Orlit post; next to the A228 north of **Hoo St Werburgh**; by **Martello Tower No. 3** at **Folkestone**; and behind the small cemetery on the B2046 south-west of **Aylesham**. Perhaps the most interesting is beside the road from **Lydd** to **Camber**, on the western edge of **Lydd Range**. This post is believed to be one of the last built and is probably the only example of an above-ground 'underground' post. Built at ground level, it has a great mound of shingle over it.

Underground monitoring posts were sited approx-imately eight miles apart in Kent so there is always one quite close anywhere in the county. Map refer-ences for all posts are given in Derek Woods's *Attack Warning Red, the History of the ROC* (see bibliogra-phy).

The Second World War ROC Group Headquarters for No. 1 Group was a Victorian house in **Maidstone** with its cellar converted to a plotting room. Later, an underground HQ was built in the back garden com-plete with generators, air filtration and decontamina-tion facilities, plotting room, canteen, dormitories, telephone exchange and radio.

WHERE TO GO
IF TIME IS SHORT

One of the best examples of a coastal defence battery is Martello Battery at **Sheerness** (TQ 909 756). The battery features concrete towers and an observation post with hipped roof. New Tavern Fort at **Gravesend** (TQ 653 742) is a remarkably complete two-gun 6-inch battery.

Anti-aircraft defences are best represented by the 3.7-inch batteries at **Erith** (TQ 534 774) and **Dover** (TR 297 400). There is a light anti-aircraft emplacement on the roof of a pillbox at **Hawkinge airfield** (TR 208 389) and a Bofors tower and Chain Home radar station at **Dunkirk** (TR 073 593 and TR 078 590 respectively). The Chain Home radar station at **Swingate**, Dover (TR 335 428), and the sound mirrors at **Capel**, **Hythe** and **Greatstone** (TR 270 386, TR 132 346, and TR 077216 respectively) are also well worth visiting.

The best examples of anti-tank defences are the Type 28 pillbox and the pillboxes built into the railway bridge at **Adisham** (TR 225 546 and TR 230 543 respectively). The pillboxes of the GHQ Line at **Teston** (TQ 710 535) and along the hill behind **Folkestone** (TR 240 378) are worthy of note and so, too, is the anti-tank wall at **Walmer** (TR 375 500). Anti-tank pimples remain at **Court-at-Street** (TR 095 768) and **Dover Castle** (TR 323 422). Other pillboxes survive around Hawkinge airfield and one of these (TR 208 389) has a light anti-aircraft emplacement on its roof.

Opposite
A 9.2-inch gun; Citadel Battery, Dover (author's collection)

Above
The 6-inch battery with guns replaced at New Tavern Fort, Gravesend

Right
The same 9.2-inch gun emplacement, 1996. Note holdfast bolts

There are few remnants of civil defence measures. An ARP warden's post lingers at **Dover Priory** station (TR 314 414) and there are semi-sunken shelters at **Lympne** (TR 115 355). Surface shelters remain at **Reinden Wood**, Hawkinge airfield's dispersed accommodation site.

CONCLUSION

The majority of sites mentioned in this volume are visible from public rights of way but many are on private land and visitors should take every precaution to avoid trespass. Most landowners are very pleased to grant access on request but a polite letter written in advance of any visit invariably makes them more amenable.

Some of the structures described here are on Ministry of Defence land and it is particularly important to obtain the permission of your local Defence Land Agent or Garrison Commander before trying to visit them. Please bear in mind that uninvited visitors, especially those seen taking photographs near active bases, may be reported as potential threats to the security of military personnel and questioned accordingly.

Finally, the majority of military defensive structures were built to fulfil an immediate need and then abandoned or even partially demolished. Whilst they may look robust, it is unwise to allow children to climb over them unsupervised or to trust to the security of any fixtures and fittings.

With a few sensible precautions, study of Britain's recent military archaeology can be a rewarding and absorbing pastime. We hope that this small volume will encourage your interest and that you will want to acquire others in the series.

Opposite

The 6-inch gun emplacements at Cliffe Fort are in more typical condition

BIBLIOGRAPHY

Anon,   *Kent Airfields in the Battle of Britain,* Kent Aviation Historical Research Society/Meresborough Books (1981)

Brooks, R J,   *Kent Airfields Remembered,* Countryside, Newbury (1990)

Collyer, D,   *East Kent at War in Old Photographs,* Sutton, Stroud (1994)

Collyer, D,   *Buzz Bomb Diary,* Kent Aviation Historical Research Society (1994)

Gander, T,   *Military Archaeology,* PSL, Sparkford (1979)

Gulvin, K,   *Kent Home Guard,* North Kent Books (1980)

Hayward, J,   *Shingle Street,* LTM Publishing (1994)

Innes, G Buchan,
               British Airfield Buildings of the Second World War, Midland, Earl Shilton (1995)

Lampe, D,   *The Last Ditch,* Cassell, London (1968)

Lowry, B (Ed),
               20th Century Defences in Britain, Council for British Archaeology (1995)

Ramsey, W G (Ed),
               'The Cross-Channel Guns', After the Battle No. 29 (1980)

Saunders, A D,
               Fortress Britain, Beaufort, (1989)

Scarth, R N,   *Mirrors by the Sea,* Hythe Civic Society (1995)

Smith, V T C,
               Defending London's River, North Kent Books (1985)

Turner, F R,   *The Maunsell Sea Forts, Part 1: The Army Forts,* Turner (1994)

Turner, F R,   *The Maunsell Sea Forts, Part 2: The Navy Forts,* Turner (1995)

Wills, H,   *Pillboxes: A Study of UK Defences 1940,* Secker & Warburg, London (1985)

Wood, D,   *Attack Warning Red,* Carmichael & Sweet (1992)

GAZETTEER

AIRFIELDS

Bekesbourne, First World War with Belfast truss hangar extant	TR 205 553
Detling	TR 802 588
Hawkinge, Expansion Period; museum	TR 215 395
Hawkinge's dispersed accommodation site	TR 215 410
Lashenden advanced landing ground	TQ 847 429
Lympne	TR 119 347
Manston, museum	TR 330 660
West Malling	TQ 678 555

ANTI-AIRCRAFT SITES

Brookland, Royal Observer Corps Orlit and underground posts	TQ 989 255
Capel, sound mirror	TR 270 386
Dover, 3.7-inch anti-aircraft battery	TR 297 400
Dover, Chain Home radar station	TR 335 428
Dunkirk, Bofors tower	TR 078 593
Dymchurch, Royal Observer Corps underground post	TR 105 315
Erith, 3.7-inch anti-aircraft battery	TQ 534 774
Folkestone, Royal Observer Corps underground posts	TR 240 367
Greatstone, sound mirrors	TR 077 216
Ham Street, Royal Observer Corps Second World War and underground posts	TR 009 331
Hawkinge, light anti-aircraft emplacement on pillbox	TR 208 389
Hoo St Werburgh, Royal Observer Corps underground post	TQ 778 735
Hythe, sound mirror	TR 132 346
Lydd, Royal Observer Corps underground post	TR 026 199
Offshore anti-aircraft forts	N/A
Orpington, Royal Observer Corps underground post	TQ 472 614

ANTI-TANK DEFENCES

Adisham, Type 28 pillbox	TR 225 546
Barfrestone, anti-tank pimples and road block sockets	TR 250 502
Court-at-Street, anti-tank pimples	TR 095 352
Dover, anti-tank gun emplacement	TR 317 429
Dover Castle, anti-tank pimples	TR 323 422
Dover Castle, 6pdr anti-tank gun position in wall	TR 325 417
Graveney Marsh, anti-tank cubes	TR 061 646
Kingsdown, camouflaged anti-tank gun emplacement	TR 379 483
Teston, GHQ Line pillboxes	TQ 710 535
Walmer, anti-tank wall	TR 375 500

CIVIL DEFENCE

Dover, ARP wardens' post	TR 314 414
Erith, surface shelters	TQ 534 774
Hawkinge, surface shelters and gas decontamination building	TR 215 410
Lympne, semi-sunken shelters	TR 115 355

COASTAL DEFENCE

Cliffe Fort, Brennan torpedo launch rails	TR 706 768
Dover Castle, Port War Signal Station	TR 327 416
Dover, Citadel Battery, 9.2-inch	TR 303 403
Dover, Langdon Battery, 6-inch and 9.2-inch	TR 339 424
Dover, St Martin's Battery, 6-inch	TR 314 407
Dymchurch, 6-inch	TR 129 321
Eastchurch, Fletcher Battery, 9.2-inch	TR 053 677
Folkestone, XDO post and Copt Point Battery, 6-inch	TR 240 367
Gillingham, Royal Engineers' Museum (Brennan torpedo)	N/A
Grain Tower, battery and boom anchorage	TR 899 760
Gravesend, New Tavern Fort, 6-inch battery	TQ 653 742
Sheerness, Martello Battery, 4.7-inch	TQ 909 756
Shellness, XDO post	TR 053 677
St Margaret's at Cliffe, South Foreland Battery, 9.2-inch	TR 359 437

PILLBOXES

A249 Maidstone–Sheppey, square First World War pillbox	TQ 851 618
Adisham, built into railway bridge	TR 230 543
Adisham, Type 28	TR 225 546
Bekesbourne, built into railway bridge	TR 191 560
Bekesbourne, Type 24	TR 200 550
Court-at-Street, garage converted to pillbox	TR 095 352
Dover, Citadel Battery, Types 23 and 24	TR 303 403
Dover, Fort Burgoyne, First World War circular pillbox	TR 323 427
Dover, St Martin's Battery, Type 23s	TR 314 407
Erith, Type 22s	TQ 534 774
Folkestone, line of Type 22s	TR 240 378
Hawkinge, Types 22 and 24 and Pickett-Hamilton	TR 215 395
Hoo St Werburgh, Type 24	TQ 778 735
GHQ Line	N/A
Teston, GHQ Line	TQ 710 535
Walmer, enhanced Type 24	TR 375 500

Kent county map

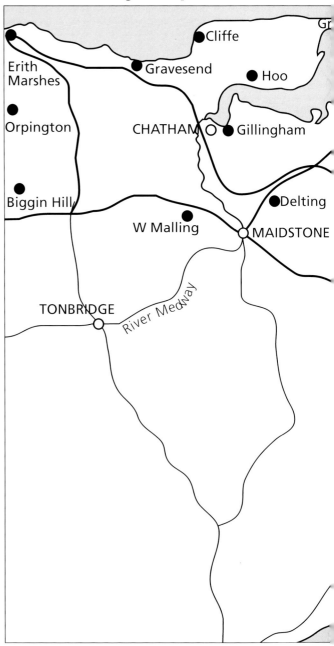

THE
DEFENCE
OF
BRITAIN

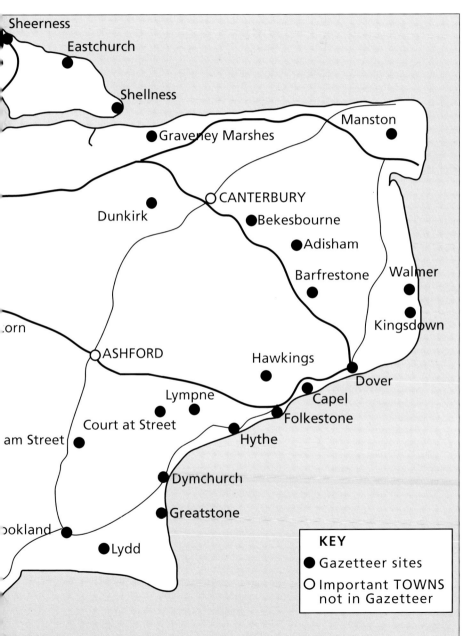

Sheerness

Eastchurch

Shellness

Graveney Marshes

Manston

CANTERBURY

Dunkirk

Bekesbourne

Adisham

Barfrestone

Walmer

Kingsdown

ASHFORD

Hawkings

Dover

Lympne

Capel

Court at Street

Folkestone

am Street

Hythe

Dymchurch

Greatstone

ookland

Lydd

orn

KEY

● Gazetteer sites

○ Important TOWNS not in Gazetteer